A World of Food

MEXICO

Geoff Barker

CLARA
HOUSE
BOOKS

Minneapolis

First published in 2010 by Clara House Books, an imprint of The Oliver Press, Inc.

Copyright © 2010 Arcturus Publishing Limited

Clara House Books
5707 West 36th Street
Minneapolis, MN 55416
USA

Produced by Arcturus Publishing Limited

Series concept: Alex Woolf
Editor: Alex Woolf
Designer: Jane Hawkins
Map Illustrator: Stefan Chabluk
Picture researcher: Alex Woolf

Picture Credits
Art Archive: 6.
César Rincón: 26.
Corbis: cover and 4 (Bob Krist), 8 (Blaine Harrington III), 10 (Patrick Ward), 11 (Lynsey Addario), 12 (Sergio Dorantes), 14 (Mario Guzman/epa), 19 *left* (Rose Hartman), 20 (Ulises Ruiz/EFE), 21 *left* (Keith Dannemiller), 22 (Liba Taylor), 25 *mole poblano* (Mark Dye/Star Ledger), 27 *top* (Macduff Everton).
Getty Images: 13 (Joanne Ciccarello/Christian Science Monitor), 15 (Jose Cabezas/AFP), 16 (Susana Gonzalez), 18 (Hector Mata/AFP), 23 (Clive Streeter), 28 (Mario Vazquez/AFP), 29 bottom (David Blumenfeld).
Saudi Aramco World/SAWDIA: 24.
Shutterstock: 3 *chili powder* (Craig McAteer), 7 *milk* (Jozsef Szasz-Fabian), 7 *vanilla beans* (Fribus Ekaterina), 7 *sugar bowl* (Danny Smythe), 7 *broken egg* (Elena Schweitzer), 7 *flan* (tacar), 9 *top* (Grigory Kubatyan), 9 *bottom* (Alexandr Vlassyuk), 17 *onion* (Marcio Maitan Alberico), 17 *lemon* (Astronom), 17 *tomato* (Dmitry Kosterev), 17 *chili powder* (Lagrima), 17 *coriander* (Pefkos), 17 and 27 *avocados* (Oliver Hoffmann), 17 *guacamole* (Cathleen Clapper), 19 *right* (Alex Staroseltsev), 21 *right* (Azucar!), 22 *peppers* (Yellowj), 24 *chili peppers* (Vakhrushev Pavel), 25 *cinnamon, dried chili peppers* (Sandra Caldwell), 25 *coriander seeds* (elena moiseeva), 25 *chocolate* (guysal), 25 *onion* (LockStockBob), 25 *raisins* (Graca Victoria), 25 *tomato puree* (lantapix), 26 *chili* (Freddy Eliasson), 29 top (Nikolai Pozdeev).

Library of Congress Cataloging-in-Publication Data

Barker, Geoff P., 1963-
Mexico / Geoff Barker.
        p. cm. -- (A world of food)
Includes bibliographical references and index.
ISBN 978-1-934545-13-3
1. Food habits--Mexico--Juvenile literature. 2. Cookery, Mexican--Juvenile literature. 3. Mexico--Social life and customs--Juvenile literature. I. Title. II. Series.

GT2853.M6B37 2010
641.300972--dc22

                                                                                            2009039930

Dewey Decimal Classification Number: 394.1'2'0972

ISBN 978-1-934545-13-3

Printed in China

www.oliverpress.com

Contents

Introduction

Mexico has a unique blend of native American and European cultures. This rapidly developing country contains ancient ruins, colorful markets, lively cities, quiet villages, spectacular countryside – and great food.

The country

Mexico is about three times the size of Texas. It borders the United States to the north and Guatemala and Belize to the south. Its first people were Indians who arrived from North America some 20,000 years ago. Mexico became home to the ancient civilizations of the Olmecs, Maya, Zapotecs, Toltecs, and Aztecs.

▲ Mexico's colorful street markets stock a huge range of fresh food. This market is in Zaachila, Oaxaca, in southern Mexico.

The most recent of these peoples were the Aztecs, who built a powerful empire in central Mexico in the 14th century. In 1519–21, the Spanish conquered Mexico. However, Aztec influence remains strong today – more than a million people speak Nahuatl, the Aztec language.

Today's Mexicans

Mexico has a population of around 110 million. Most speak Spanish, though very few Mexicans are of pure Spanish descent. There are many *indigenas* (indigenous people), but the majority of Mexicans are mestizos – people of mixed native and Spanish ancestry.

Mexican food

You will find sweet corn in most Mexican dishes. No other country in the world uses sweet corn with as much imagination. This vegetable is thought to have originated in Mexico. Known as *elote*, it is simply roasted and sold as corn on the cob at street stalls. Ground into flour (like wheat for bread), it becomes a staple food – tortillas.

▼ This map shows the locations of some of the places mentioned in this book.

SOME COMMON MEXICAN FOODS

Spanish is the main language spoken in Mexico (although there are over 60 native languages). Here are a few Spanish food words:

Word	Pronunciation	Meaning
la comida	lah koh-MEE-dah	meal
las frutas	lass FROO-tass	fruit
las verduras	lass ver-DOO-rass	vegetables
la carne	lah KAHR-nay	meat
el pescado	el pess-KAH-do	fish
los huevos	loss WAY-voss	eggs
el jamón	el ham-ON	ham
la tortilla	lah tor-TEE-yah	tortilla
la mole	lah MO-lay	sauce
la guacamole	lah gwah-cah-MO-lay	guacamole

History

The early Mexicans farmed a wide range of crops, including sweet corn, beans, chilies, peppers, tomatoes, pumpkins, peanuts, and avocados. These foods continue to dominate Mexican food. Other cooking ingredients and flavorings still used today include chocolate and vanilla.

European foods

In the 16th century, Europeans brought livestock with them such as chickens, goats, and pigs. They also introduced new cooking ingredients such as wheat and rice, and flavorings such as garlic and cinnamon. Apples, oranges, and peaches, as well as cheese, milk, and eggs, were introduced to Mexican food.

Flan

Flan is a similar dish to the French crème caramel, or British baked custards. This melt-in-the-mouth dessert was originally brought over to Mexico by Spanish conquerors.

▶ Hernando Cortés (center, seated at table) was a Spanish conqueror of Mexico. Here he holds a banquet for supporters of the last king of the Aztecs, Montezuma.

RECIPE: flan

Equipment
- 6 small molds • 2 small pans • wooden spoon
- large bowl • large shallow ovenproof dish • knife

Ingredients
- vegetable oil • 1 cup (200g) sugar
- 2 cups (500ml) milk • vanilla extract
- 3 eggs • 2 egg yolks

1 Preheat oven to 300°F (150°C). Lightly grease the molds with oil.

2 Put half the sugar and 1 tablespoon of water in a pan. Heat gently, stirring all the time.

3 When melted, pour to cover the bottom of each mold. Cool.

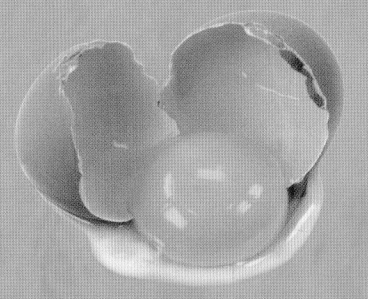

4 Put milk and a few drops of vanilla in another pan. Bring to a boil.

5 Beat remaining sugar, eggs, and egg yolks together in a bowl. Gradually stir in the milk. Pour the custard mix into each mold.

6 Put each filled mold into the dish. Ask a grown-up to pour hot water around each mold to come halfway up the sides. Cook in the oven for about 40 minutes.

7 Carefully remove molds from the oven and from the dish. Cool, then chill for about 3 hours. Use a knife to loosen the edge of each custard and turn upside down on a serving plate.

Climate and Soil

Some parts of Mexico are mountainous, with snowy peaks and a chilly climate. The low-lying coastal areas to the south, west, and east of the country are much warmer. The climate here varies from arid desert to lush tropical.

Land of contrasts

Northern Mexico is mainly hot, dry desert with little rainfall. By contrast, the lower-lying southern regions have a tropical climate. The Yucatán Peninsula, in the south, has hot and humid weather. Its land is suitable for growing tropical fruits, such as pineapples, coconuts, and papayas.

Mountainous landscape

A large part of Mexico is mountainous, and almost half the country is over 5,000 feet above sea level. The snow-capped volcanic peaks of Popocatepetl and

▼ The Copper Canyon consists of six great canyons in the northwest of Mexico.

▲ Xochimilco is in Mexico City. Its boats form a floating market.

SWEET CORN

Sweet corn comes from the maize family of plants. It grows best in well-drained, sandy soil and in hot, dry temperatures. Corn is not just a tasty food – it is used in toothpaste, glues, shoe polish, and even to make the fuel ethanol.

Iztacchihuatl ("Popo" and "Izta") are more than 17,000 feet high and form a natural barrier between Mexico City and Puebla.

High central plateau

Mexico is dominated by two mountain ranges that run north to south: the Western and Eastern Sierra Madre. Between these two great ranges is a large, fertile valley running up the middle of the country. This central plateau has a mild climate with warm summers and cool winters. Southern parts of the plateau have humid summers. They can receive heavy rainfall and floods.

Soil

In the arid north, the land has been overgrazed by cattle. Livestock have flattened any vegetation and the thin layer of topsoil has been lost. Wooded land has also been deforested, causing soil erosion. In the southern regions, the soil is very fertile and ideal for growing a variety of crops.

Farming

In Mexico, most people living in the country are farmers. Families tend to keep animals such as chickens, pigs, and goats. Typical small farms might grow sweet corn, beans, and potatoes to sell at market and to feed their families.

Farms

Most small farmers do not have mechanized equipment to farm the land. They use simple hoes, or plows pulled by animals. Larger farms are more likely to use modern machinery, such as tractors, and sprinkler systems to water the crops. They grow crops such as wheat, coffee, and sugar cane. These types of crops, as well as fruit and vegetables, are grown for export.

▲ Mexican farmers work very hard on the land. Most still use animals, such as mules or horses, to pull their plows.

Ranching

In northern Mexico, the hot, dry land is unsuitable for growing many crops. Instead, cattle are reared for meat on a huge scale. Beef is a popular food in the north of Mexico, but is also sold to the United States. In southern Mexico, cattle are more commonly raised to make dairy products such as milk and cheese.

CAUGHT!

Red snappers are reef fish found in the Gulf of Mexico. The fish mature by the time they are two years old. A ten-year-old female fish is able to produce 60 million eggs every year. Most eggs and young snapper fish die. Of the 60 million eggs produced, perhaps only 450 might survive to reach a length of 2 inches. When harvested, most snappers are up to 20 inches long.

Fishing

The coastal parts of Mexico are highly dependent on fishing. From the Pacific Ocean in the west to the Gulf of Mexico and Caribbean Sea in the east, Mexico has more than 7,000 miles of coastline. Over a quarter of a million people work in the fishing industry. Most of the catch comes from the Pacific Ocean. The main commercial catches are shrimp, tuna, lobster, and anchovies. Bass, sardines, abalone, tilapia, snapper, and mackerel are also all harvested from the sea.

▶ Two fishermen load a haul of large squid onto the dock at Guaymas, Mexico, on the Gulf of California.

Culture

Mexicans eat three meals a day – breakfast, lunch, and supper. Traditionally, they eat at home, but they also enjoy visiting restaurants. Eating out with friends and family is a very popular pastime in Mexico.

Hearty appetites

Mexican people start the day with *desayuno*, or breakfast. This might be sweet pastries or rolls washed down with coffee. Or they might have a snack of tacos – tortillas rolled around a filling of cheese, beans, and meat. Some have a more substantial snack in the middle of the morning with *huevos rancheros* – fried egg with salsa on tortilla.

▼ Mexican families like to share good food at home. A favorite dish is steam-cooked *tamales* (see page 26).

Changing customs

Traditionally, the most filling meal of the day is lunch. People dining out eat the *comida corrida*, or main meal. A typical meal may consist of soup, followed by a plate of pasta, vegetables and beans, then a dessert. Supper is usually light and may be eaten quite late. However, for city-dwellers, customs are changing, and increasing numbers enjoy their main meal in the evening.

Siesta time

In Mexico, people traditionally have a siesta, or afternoon nap. After a hard morning's work and a filling lunch, many Mexicans like to lie down to rest. This habit makes a lot of sense as this is typically the hottest part of the day.

Eating out

For well-to-do Mexicans, the cities have many upscale restaurants. Those with less money or time opt for tasty tortilla snacks such as enchiladas, burritos, or chimichangas from *taquerias*, or street stalls.

▼ A worker fills taco shells at a *taqueria* in Mexico City.

TORTILLA

Tortillas are the basis of many, many Mexican dishes. They are made from corn. The corn is allowed to dry, then it is ground into flour. Like a flatbread pancake, a tortilla can be rolled, stuffed, layered, or fried. There are many different variations. Tortilla chips and tacos (large crispy shells for different fillings) are favorites all over the world. This versatile bread is very popular in the United States. More tortillas are sold there than any other ethnic type of bread, including bagels and pita breads.

Religion

Mexico has no official religion, but most Mexicans are Roman Catholics. Spanish conquerors arrived nearly 500 years ago, bringing their religion. Roman Catholicism has had a great impact on the country and on the Mexican way of life.

Spanish influence

Mexico was ruled by the Spanish as the colony of "New Spain" for almost 300 years. During this time, traditional dishes containing sweet corn, beans, chilies, and avocados remained popular, but there were also changes. Mexicans started to consume the new foods that the Spanish had brought into the country. As well as eating more meat, including chicken and pork, Mexicans began to enjoy versatile ingredients such as eggs and milk in many new dishes, including *huevos rancheros* and *flan*.

Food at Lent

The new religion from Spain brought different beliefs and customs. This affected what Mexicans ate on different occasions, for example during Roman Catholic festivals such as Easter and Christmas. Mexicans

▶ In a special ceremony, fish is blessed on a Friday at the Metropolitan Cathedral in Mexico City. The blessing is carried out to encourage Mexicans to eat fish during Lent.

▲ Visitors to a shrine to the Virgin Mary receive pork and rice soup. This food is given as part of the preparations for the Flower and Palm Festival early in May.

TABLECLOTH STAINS

A popular Mexican dish served during the Festival of Corpus Christi is *mancha manteles*, which means "tablecloth stainer." The dish consists of turkey, sausages, tomatoes, chilies, and cinnamon, usually combined with fruits such as pineapples and apples. If you spill any of the brick-red sauce, you will see how it gets its strange name.

began to give up certain foods during Lent, known as La Cueresma. This is a period of 40 days before Easter Sunday, from Ash Wednesday to Holy Saturday.

Catholic Mexicans typically give up meat during this period. Fish is a popular substitute for meat at this time. There are also many specially made meat-free dishes. These include potato or cauliflower croquettes, or fritters, shrimp soup, tomato soup, and green vegetables in a tasty sauce. *Capirotada*, or bread pudding, makes a tasty and filling dessert.

Old roots remain

Despite the dominance of Roman Catholicism in Mexico, some pagan customs persist. Even today, every town and village in Mexico has its own special fiestas (festivals). These events demonstrate the importance of food in everyday life, and their origins go back to pre-Christian times. Typically these fiestas celebrate the arrival of rains for the crops or the harvest itself.

Semana Santa

The Catholic calendar provides the people of Mexico with opportunities for colorful celebrations and festivals throughout the year. One of the most important is Holy Week, or Semana Santa, before Easter.

There is a festive atmosphere in Mexico from Holy Thursday to Resurrection Sunday. Streets come alive as people go out to meet family and friends and celebrate Easter together. There are Passion plays and religious processions, when figures dressed as Christ drag a cross through crowds of onlookers.

Children and adults enjoy ice cream and shaved ices – cool, refreshing drinks made from fresh fruit juices. There are also special Easter treats such as small hot cakes topped with marmalade, and savory *pambazos* – filled rolls soaked in tomato salsa (sauce).

◀ Every year during Holy Week, or Semana Santa, Mexicans take part in special plays and processions. They act out scenes from the life of Jesus, for example when Jesus was imprisoned by Roman soldiers.

Guacamole

Avocado trees are abundant in Mexico, and guacamole is a simple dish made from avocados. Guacamole is eaten throughout Mexico during Holy Week. However, it is not just a festival food but is eaten with almost every Mexican meal. This tasty fresh green purée is delicious spread as a filling on tortillas or as an accompaniment to meat dishes.

RECIPE: guacamole

Equipment
- knife • bowl • spoon • fork

Ingredients
- 1 small onion • 1 large tomato
- handful of fresh cilantro
- ½ fresh chili or ¼ teaspoon chili powder (optional)
- 2 large ripe avocados • 1 tablespoon lemon juice
- salt and pepper, to taste

Ask a grown-up to help you with the chopping.

1 Peel the onion and finely chop. Chop the tomato, removing the seeds.

2 Finely chop the cilantro. Put the chopped onion, tomato, and cilantro in a bowl. If you want a spicier flavor, chop some fresh chili and mix in.

3 Cut the avocados carefully in half lengthways. Use a spoon to remove the pit, then scoop out the flesh into the bowl.

4 Add the lemon juice and a little salt and pepper. Mash the ingredients together with a fork.

La Guelaguetza

The festival of La Guelaguetza takes place every July in the state of Oaxaca in southern Mexico. The name means an offering or gift by the people to the gods. It comes from an ancient custom of thanking the gods for rains and a good harvest.

▲ Food plays an important part in the celebrations of the Guelaguetza. Special Oaxacan dishes are served.

Hilltop celebrations

The origins of La Guelaguetza go back 3,000 years. The original celebrations centered on a hill overlooking the city of Oaxaca. They emphasized the importance of corn, the staple of the Mexican Indians' diet. Customs have changed over the years. The Spanish moved the date of the fiesta to July 16 to combine it with the Catholic feast of the Virgin of Carmen. In recent years, the two Mondays following the Feast of Carmen are set aside for festivities for La Guelaguetza.

Huge spectacle

Today, celebrations take place all over the state of Oaxaca. The largest Guelaguetza is near the city of Oaxaca itself. The city has a huge outdoor arena that holds about 11,000 people. It puts on a lively spectacle that includes folk music, colorful dance, and shows of legends.

People still remember the importance of corn, and every year a "Corn Goddess" is chosen as queen of the fiesta. One of the highlights is the exotic Flor de Piña, or Flower of the Pineapple dance. Female dancers carry pineapples on their shoulders. At the end of the show, they throw their fruit into the crowd.

FLOWER FRUIT

Huge quantities of pineapples are grown in Mexico, especially in Veracruz. Most are eaten locally – only five percent are exported. A pineapple is not really a single fruit. It is in fact a collection of a 100 or more separate flowers that grow in the middle of a cactus-like plant. As each flower grows and swells up with juice, the whole cluster of tiny fruits becomes the pineapple "fruit."

◀ Women in traditional colorful clothing perform the Flower of the Pineapple dance at the Guelaguetza festival in Oaxaca.

Day of the Dead

Mexico is famous for a festival known as the Day of the Dead, held each year at the beginning of November. Mexicans honor dead family and friends in a unique celebration of life and death.

The Day of the Dead is often thought of as a lively public spectacle, but for many Mexicans it is a private affair. Some celebrate the occasion at the graves of loved ones, others at home.

Before the Day of the Dead, many Mexicans build private altars in their homes, where they make special offerings to the dead. They adorn these home-made shrines with candles, photos, and orange marigold flowers. Favorite drinks and foods, such as pumpkin sweets and bread, are also laid out to persuade the spirits of loved ones to return to their family once more.

Visiting family graves

Celebrations vary around Mexico, but in rural areas most families visit local cemeteries. Some spend all night beside relatives' graves, which they adorn with candles,

◀ Graveyards are lit with candles all night during the Day of the Dead festival. People put flowers and special offerings on the graves.

▲ A woman in Xochimilco, Mexico City, prepares *pan de muertos* at the market. She glazes the top of the bread with egg so that it looks shiny after baking.

marigolds, and foods. Perhaps the most important food is the sweet egg bread, *pan de muertos*. This "bread of the dead" is usually round, with bone-shaped pieces of bread stuck on top. Sometimes the bread is skull-shaped. It is part of a family picnic to share with the dead.

Street celebrations

People in towns and cities often take part in more lively street festivities, including eating and drinking. Street stalls sell decorated iced sugar skulls and the orange-scented "bread of the dead."

SKULLS OF SUGAR

Edible iced sugar skulls are a big part of the Day of the Dead festival. People can buy these colorfully decorated skulls from local street stalls. They form part of the foods taken to the graves of dead relatives. Some are already iced with Mexican names, so people can buy a ready-made, personalized sweet skull.

▲ People use clay molds to make the skulls, which are painted with colored icing.

Our Lady of Guadalupe

The Day of Our Lady of Guadalupe is one of the most important religious holidays in Mexico. Each year on December 12 there are huge fiestas throughout Mexico and Central America to honor the Virgin Mary, mother of Jesus.

The Queen of Mexico

The festival originates from 1531, when the Virgin Mary is said to have appeared to a poor Aztec Indian called Juan Diego. The 16th-century image of the Virgin Mary is one of the most important religious symbols for Mexicans. Today, many Mexicans make a

▲ Every year, musicians play at the Guadalupe festival in Mexico City. They celebrate the day in 1531 when the Virgin Mary appeared in front of a Mexican peasant.

special trip to the Basilica de Guadalupe in Mexico City to honor Our Lady of Guadalupe. Other Mexicans make *posadas*, or processions, to their own local church to pray. Most carry images of the Virgin. Fireworks, songs, and traditional dances honor La Reina de Mexico, the "Queen of Mexico."

Special feast day

Many Mexican people save up during the year to be able to afford to celebrate this religious occasion in style. The Feast of Our Lady of Guadalupe, celebrated on December 12, also marks the beginning of the Christmas season.

The feast might start with spinach soup with macaroni. Main dishes are likely to include rice and black beans, chicken in spiced chocolate sauce (*mole poblano*), and tacos served with guacamole. Other traditional Mexican foods, such as enchiladas, burritos, and *tamales* (see page 26) are also popular choices. A favorite dessert at the feast is *flan* (baked custard). Milky coffee is served after the food.

BISCUITS FOR THE FEAST

Many Mexican households bake *bizcochos*, or biscuits, for December 12. They often form the dough into special flower shapes, then the biscuits are dipped into cinnamon-flavored sugar before baking. Mexicans also enjoy *bizcochos* throughout Christmas. Adults might have a glass of wine with them, while children love them with hot chocolate.

▼ Among favorite Mexican sweet biscuits and pastries are "ears" and "shells."

No visit to Mexico is complete without sampling the local delicacies. Mexican cuisine varies from region to region, but perhaps the first place to start is a one-hour bus ride away from Mexico City, in the city of Puebla.

Special chocolate sauce

Mole poblano is a spiced chocolate sauce used as an accompaniment for turkey, and many regard it as Mexico's national dish. It is in fact a speciality of Puebla – its name means "sauce from Puebla."

The sauce is thought to have been invented in the 16th century by the nuns of the Convent of Santa Rosa in Puebla. According to legend, the Spanish viceroy was due to visit their convent. Finding they had nothing to serve him, they prayed for inspiration. An angel appeared and, under his guidance, they created the sauce.

▶ Mole poblano is said to have been invented here in the kitchen of the Convent of Santa Rosa in Puebla.

RECIPE: *mole poblano*

Equipment
- frying pan • measuring cups • sieve
- knife • food processor or blender

Ingredients
- 4 small dried chili peppers
- 1 small cinnamon stick
- 1 teaspoon coriander seeds
- 1 teaspoon anise seeds
- 3 tablespoons (50g) sesame seeds
- 3 tablespoons (50g) blanched almonds
- 3 tablespoons (50g) raisins • 1 onion
- 2 tablespoons (30ml) tomato purée
- 2 tablespoons (30ml) oil
- 3 tablespoons (50g) dark chocolate pieces
- 1 cup (250ml) stock or gravy

Ask a grown-up to help you with the
toasting, chopping, and frying.

1 Toast the chili, cinnamon stick, coriander, and anise
seeds in a dry pan for a minute. Cover with 1½ cups
(350ml) boiling water and leave for 1 hour. Strain the liquid,
set aside the water and the chilies. Remove the chili seeds.

2 Put sesame seeds, almonds, and raisins in a food processor.
Peel and chop the onion. Add onion and tomato purée to
food processor, along with chilies. Blend until smooth
(adding some water if too thick).

3 Heat oil in the frying pan. Add the chili
mixture and heat. Add the chocolate and
melt. Stir in the stock or gravy gradually.

4 Coat hot, cooked slices of turkey with the
chocolate sauce.

25

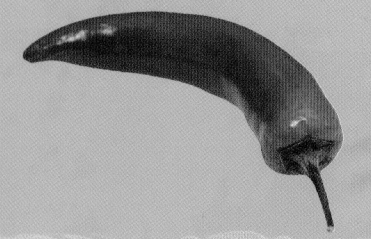

Regional Cuisines

Tortillas, guacamole, beans, chilies, and sweet corn are favorites throughout Mexico. However, each region has its own specialty, from meat-based dishes in the north to southern fried grasshoppers.

Cuisine of the north

Northern Mexico is very dry, so the land is not suitable for growing crops. Huge cattle ranches provide large quantities of beef. Grilled or barbecued meat (*asado*) is very popular. One regional speciality is *cabrito asado*, or whole roasted baby goat. This meat feast is served up in big portions with tortillas and salsa.

Southern regions

In the fertile valleys and highlands of Central Mexico, people use a range of ingredients in their dishes, including wild mushrooms, squash, and pumpkin. *Tamales* are a traditional dish in the state of Hidalgo. These steam-cooked corn-dough "biscuits" are stuffed with tasty ingredients such as pork, cheese, or beans.

▼ If you are in Oaxaca, try the crunchy fried grasshoppers.

In Oaxaca in southern Mexico, fresh vegetables, fruit, and herbs and spices grow in abundance. Locals enjoy enormous tortillas filled with beans and the local stringy cheese. *Chapulines* are crunchy fried grasshoppers flavored with chili and lime.

▲ The many restaurants on Mexico's coastline offer tourists a varied fish and seafood menu as well as beautiful, sunny beaches.

AVOCADOS

Avocados are popular throughout the country and they probably originated in southern Mexico. Avocados are usually pear shaped and are also known as avocado pears. Some call them "alligator pears" due to the rough, leathery skin of some varieties. They may taste like vegetables, but avocados are actually fruits. The fruit is not the only part of the plant used for food. In some parts of Mexico, avocado tree leaves are used as a flavoring for stews.

Food from the coast

Fish and seafood are, of course, favorites in coastal regions. A popular dish from Veracruz, on the Gulf of Mexico, is baby octopus. Another is *pescado a la Veracruzana* (fish of Veracruz), in which fish is cooked in a sauce of tomatoes, onions, garlic, olives, chilies, and other spices.

The Yucatán

Hot and tropical, the Yucatán is a mainly fertile region in southeastern Mexico. Its food looks back to Mayan traditions, based on corn, beans, and meat. The cuisine here is also influenced by spicy Caribbean flavors and contains tropical fruits.

Mexican food is hugely popular across much of the world. But what we may think of as Mexican cuisine is often an Americanized version of the country's food – in some cases, it isn't Mexican at all.

▲ In Toluca, Mexico, a group of Mazahuas (an indigenous Mexican people) try to tempt customers in a fast-food restaurant with some of their traditional cuisine.

Modern Mexican cuisine really began after the Spanish conquest, as European foods flooded into Mexico. The arrival of chickens, pigs, goats, and cattle introduced more meat into the Mexican diet, as well as dairy products. Corn remained the staple grain, but rice also grew in importance. At the same time, Mexico's home-grown foods, such as sweet corn, chilies, tomatoes, avocados, vanilla, and chocolate began to gain popularity in Europe and elsewhere.

Tex-Mex

Five hundred years later, Mexican food is more popular than ever. Ask people to name a classic Mexican dish and many will say chili con carne. However, this spicy, meaty stew is not Mexican at all – it is really an American dish, or "Tex-Mex." Tex-Mex food comes from the Texas-Mexico border region. You may find chili con carne on the menu in Mexican restaurants – but only in the areas frequented by tourists.

Mexican style

The American fast-food restaurant chain Taco Bell specializes in Mexican-style cuisine. It has around 5,800 restaurants in the United States and has opened restaurants in Canada, Europe, Asia, South America, and even in Mexico itself. However, the company admits that its brand has more to do with "quick service and good value" than true Mexican food.

Today, traditional Mexican cuisine can be enjoyed in many of the world's major cities. However, the best way to sample Mexican food is to visit Mexico.

CHOC-TASTIC!

When Cortés arrived at Tenochtitlan (today's Mexico City) in the early 16th century, he was presented with a special drink by the Aztec emperor Montezuma. It was a combination of the local ingredients of cocoa beans, vanilla, and honey – a tasty hot chocolate drink. Chocolate has been a hit around the world ever since.

▼ Mexican-style food is popular all over the world.

Glossary

ancestry The people from whom someone is descended.

civilization A society with an advanced culture and a high level of social organization.

cuisine A style or way of cooking, usually from a particular region.

custom A long-established habit or tradition.

descent The path from an ancestor.

erosion The act of wearing away, or eroding.

ethanol A type of alcohol, used as a fuel.

export Sell goods to a foreign country.

fertile Able to produce an abundance of plants.

fiestas Religious festivals, celebrations or feasts.

humid Moist or damp.

indigenous Native.

livestock Cattle, horses, pigs, or other animals kept on a farm.

Maya Indian people from Yucatán and other regions of Central America, who had an advanced civilization before the Spanish conquest.

overgraze Graze land so much that it has lost nourishment, or is destroyed.

pagan Having ancient religious beliefs, not related to Christianity, Islam, or Judaism.

Passion plays Plays depicting the Passion, or suffering and death, of Christ.

peninsula A narrow piece of land that juts out from the mainland into the sea.

plateau An elevated, mainly level area of land.

salsa A spicy, uncooked sauce, usually consisting of tomatoes, onions and chilies.

shrine A holy or sacred place such as a tomb or place of worship.

staple A food that forms the basis of the diet of the people of a particular country or region.

topsoil The surface layer of soil.

tropical To do with the tropics, the area to the north and south of the equator. Also describes very hot and humid weather.

versatile Describing something that can be adapted for many uses.

viceroy The governor of a colony or country who rules in the name of his king or queen, or government.

volcanic Caused or produced by volcanoes.

Further Information

Books

Eyewitness Travel Guide: Mexico by Marlena Spieler (Dorling Kindersley, 2008)

Festive Food of Mexico by Elisabeth Lambert Ortiz (Kyle Cathie, 2006)

Freestyle Express: Destination Detectives: Mexico by Jen Green (Raintree, 2006)

Freestyle Express: Time Travel Guides: The Aztec Empire by Jane Bingham (Raintree, 2007)

Mexico: A World of Recipes by Julie McCulloch (Heinemann Library, 2002)

Websites

allrecipes.co.uk
This recipe website includes some Mexican favorites, such as tortillas or *pan de muertos* (bread of the dead).

www.food-links.com/countries/mexico/mexico.php
This website contains information about the food and culture of Mexico.

www.facts-about-mexico.com
This website contains general information on Mexico, including pages on its food, people, religion, and culture.

www.holidays.net/dayofthedead/
This website contains some interesting background information on Mexico's Day of the Dead.

DVDs

Globe Trekker: Ultimate Mexico (Pinnacle Vision, 2007)

Vista Point: Mexico City (TravelVideoStore.com, 2005)

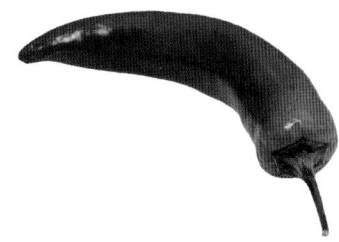

Index